MW00413111

FIRE YOURSELF

How to Overpower Your Competition, Reclaim Your Freedom,
and Triple Your Revenue in the Next 12 Months by Hiring a
Rockstar Acquisition Manager

B R I A N   E L L W O O D

© 2017 Brian Ellwood
All rights reserved.

ISBN: 0692887350
ISBN 13: 9780692887356

TABLE OF CONTENTS

INTRODUCTION

WHAT THIS BOOK IS, AND WHAT IT IS NOT

Hi! My name is Brian Ellwood. Thank you for picking up this book. I promise you that if you **take action** on what you learn here, it will do wonders for your real estate business.

I'll get into my story in a minute. But first, let's talk about what this book IS, what it IS NOT, and what you can expect to get out of it.

This book is NOT a complete sales training book for your acquisition manager. It DOES contain some very powerful tidbits that can double or triple your conversion rate when you go on appointments. But, sales as a whole is a giant topic on its own. If you want to master it, you will need to read many more books, hire sales coaches, and create and continually upgrade your "Sales Process" (explained in Chapter 5). Mostly, you'll need to get experience.

This book IS the guide that will help you:

- Easily find the right candidates to interview
- Do thorough due diligence on each candidate (interview process, contest/challenge, personality tests, etc) so that you can identify the absolute best AM (Acquisition Manager) to hire
- Develop the right pay structure for your AM, making sure that they don't ever cost you $, but only MAKE you money.

- Onboard/Train your AM to get them up and running quickly, so that you will see an immediate positive impact
- Coach your AM regularly, continuing to upgrade their skills (and thus conversion rate) each week
- Manage your AM ongoing, knowing what to expect of them and what KPI's (Key Performance Indicators) to track
- Get loads of your time back that you can apply towards marketing and high-level strategic/visionary work, the type of work that will actually grow your business (working ON, not IN, your business).

In this book, I will prove to you that having an Acquisition Manager on your team, even if they were terrible, would easily give you a 50-100% increase in yearly revenue. When we hired our first AM, his efforts TRIPLED our revenue (300%) within 12 months. He, of course, was not terrible. I'll show you what type of person to hire in Chapter 3.

As I said before, this book will teach you everything you need to know to place an AM within your business, get them going, and see fantastic results. If you want to continue to improve your results beyond that, you'll need to:

- Keep coaching your AM ongoing, raising their sales abilities
- Spend your newfound time working on marketing to drive more leads into your business, ultimately to the point where you need to hire a *second* AM
- Rinse and repeat!

This really is a simple, easy tweak that will explode your real estate investing business. Yes, it's a decent amount of grunt work up front. But once the AM is up and running, it's such a load off your shoulders. Plus, if you've never hired someone for an important position like this, or delegated duties that were eating up your time to someone else, this is great practice towards becoming a better entrepreneur. As I'll explain later, the best entrepreneurs are masters at getting results from *other people*. They don't cling to every part of their businesses.

Sound good? Ok, before we dive into the nitty gritty, here's a little background on me and how I came to make this discovery within my own business.

Note: In this book, I refer to this position as "Acquisition Manager", "AM", "rep", and "sales rep". They all mean the same thing.

Chapter 1

MY EPIPHANY

MY LIFE TODAY

My name is Brian Ellwood. I live in sunny Colorado. I have an amazing girlfriend and great family and friends. I snowboard about 30 days out of the year. I practice parkour (they have parkour gyms here!), play volleyball, lift weights, go hiking, and mountain biking. I love good beer (especially IPA's) and good coffee. I have an espresso machine at my house and make cappuccinos every morning! My friends would probably add to this that I'm pretty nerdy (and goofy) too.

I own a fix and flip business based in Middle Tennessee. We do over 70 flips per year. Our company also owns dozens of rental properties. Between the flip business and the rentals, I have enough money to live my ideal life.

I am also a real estate investing coach. I am fortunate to get to spend my day working with members of my amazing team and my coaching clients, learning, growing, teaching, and leading. I've got all I could ask for.

My true passion is teaching others how to design their lifestyle and get results through real estate investing. I want others to experience the same transformation I did. I want to show people that they don't have to be a slave to their jobs or to the structure that society tries to cram you into.

To do that, I teach them how to built automated, profitable, and conservative (meaning low-risk) real estate investing companies. Businesses that they can run **virtually** from their own home. I show them how to pick markets where the numbers make sense, build marketing and sales machines within those markets, ultimately producing deals that they can flip, hold, or both.

The ultimate goal is for my clients to end up with a portfolio of rental properties that generate enough passive income (meaning they don't have to work for it) to live their ideal lifestyle, whatever that is. Income that they can count on to support them and their families for the rest of their lives.

This is what I'm excited about. This is what I'm here to help others do.

But, for the majority of my life, things weren't nearly so great. Let's back up a bit...

MY STORY

Starting at the age of 15, I always had a job. Man, I worked everywhere. Chik-Fil-A, CVS Pharmacy, Smoothie King, Jersey Mike's, Hat World, a bowling alley, a pill packing place, mowing lawns, sealing driveways, staining fences, writing papers for people in college (probably not legal). You name it, I did it.

I graduated from the University of Tennessee in 2007 with a badass degree in....English! I then decided it would be a good idea to get a job at Nissan selling cars. The sales manager was a 50 something red-faced guy on steroids who wasn't exactly pleasant. I quit after 30 days and only sold 1 car. I hated it so much that I would go in the bathroom and hide when I saw customers enter the parking lot (and here I am writing a book about sales...bear with me a second!).

I then got a corporate job in healthcare for 3 years. I got somewhat comfortable there for a little while (worst possible scenario). But, my gut was always reminding me to get the hell out of there as soon as I could. At one point, my body literally began to ache at just the thought of going into that job. I'd lay in bed staring at the ceiling after my alarm clock went off, surprised at the fact that, in my mid twenties, I was already getting depressed.

I quit the corporate job when it became obvious that it was taking a huge toll on my mental and physical health. I went back to grad school and got 2 credits shy of a Master's Degree in Educational Counseling before I realized I was **again** going down the wrong path.

I was out of money and forced to take any job I could get. I got hired at a grocery store making 9 bucks an hour as a college graduate. Ballin! But at that point, something inside me had shifted. As I stood in the kitchen chopping up lettuce in an apron, I knew the future was going to be different. I finally realized deep down that no JOB was ever going to fulfill me. I had to create something on my own.

I started seeking answers through books, podcasts, and meeting with other people who were doing things I admired. I was desperate. I would shake hands with people who came in the grocery store and ask them what they did for a living. When I met an entrepreneur, my eyes lit up as I probed them with a ton of questions. I was really curious about how people made money without having a job.

One day I met a really cool guy in the grocery store who had a successful fix-n-flip real estate company. After I annoyed him enough times, he agreed to mentor me. He taught me how to find deals.

Finding a mentor was the best thing that ever happened to me.

A few months later, I found him a good deal. I had mailed a yellow letter to a busted up house. The seller called me and said a squatter was living there who was addicted to drugs. My mentor asked me to go take pictures of the house. The "tenant" wouldn't even let me in. He also had a scary pit bull chained up in the front yard. He agreed that if I l went and bought him Burger King breakfast he would let me inside. I still remember running through that front yard balancing a tray of orange juice and coffee, hurdling just out of reach of that pit bull! I'd pay good money for a video of that now.

I got the pictures and my mentor agreed to buy it. After the closing, he invited me to lunch. With a smile, he whipped out his checkbook, stroked a check and slid it across the table...

$1,000!

It was the biggest check I'd ever made at one time.

But what really shook me was this: I had made that check all on my own, **without** having a job.

I saw the light.

That was when I realized that we are not paid based upon how much we work. We are always paid based upon the **value** we add. If you have a job with a fixed hourly rate or a salary, it's just that your company (or the government) has **pre-decided** how much value you can add in that position, and attached a dollar figure to it. They obviously don't get it right a lot of the time either. Just look at a teacher's salary.

That really bugs me. In the entrepreneurial world, if you can produce a ton of value, you can literally make a million bucks in a day. No one cares how long it took you to produce it, as long as the value is there.

I want to get to the part of my story that's helpful for you, as it relates to the topic of this book. So, let's fast forward to about 1-2 years later...

By then, I had my own small real estate business. I was a one man show. I drove around and wrote down addresses, handwrote yellow letters, took the calls, went on appointments, and got the contracts signed. I did it all by myself.

The scariest part for me was **talking to sellers!** Man, I hated that part. Before I made phone calls, I used to put on a full pinstripe suit and tie, with dress shoes. I would pace around my house and listen to the click of my dress shoes on the wooden floors. Somehow that powerful "click" sound gave me a little boost of confidence. I also drank TONS of coffee so that I'd be amped up enough to just barely get over my fears. Those were very uncomfortable times.

If I had to do it all over again, I would have hired an AM right off the bat, so I could have skipped that stage all together. If you're in this phase or about to be in it, you've come across this book at the perfect time.

Not long after this, I met a rockstar guy named Frank and we decided to partner up 50/50. One of the main things I remember about the early days is us hanging out in my living room, doing high level strategic work to grow our business. Then the phone would ring. A customer! We would both excitedly shut our laptops, get in the car together and head to the appointment (yes we even went on appointments together), to try and get a contract signed.

We were constantly being pulled away from working ON our business. We were making money, but we had no time to strategize on how we were going to grow out of that stage.

WORKING ON VERSUS IN YOUR BUSINESS

Imagine you're mopping water up from your kitchen floor. You go around mopping forever but the water never ends. You start to develop strategies for mopping faster and more efficiently, but there's still no end to the water in sight. It almost seems to keep reappearing. Even getting worse.

One day while mopping, you happen to look up at the ceiling and see a hole! Water has been leaking in from the roof all along. And it's raining bullets outside. What do you do now?

The logical thing would be to fix the leak in the roof first, then return to mopping. The leak in the roof is the **core problem.**

But when it comes to business, entrepreneurs usually do the opposite. They ignore the leak (core problem) and keep on mopping. They don't stop mopping in order to make time to fix the CAUSE of their mopping.

Many of you are so busy sending out marketing, answering calls, going on appointments, following up with leads, getting contracts, managing renovations, and paying bills that you never have time to step OUT of that stream, see where the bottlenecks are, and strategize a way to remove yourself from it.

But, making time to work ON your business is the only way you will build a real company.

Hiring an AM and training them to replace you **is** working ON your business, not IN it.

MY LIFE BEFORE AND AFTER HIRING AN AM

Another year went by and we were busy as ever, going on appointments and taking phone calls. We decided to get some help. We hired a rockstar business coach named Joe McCall (who is now a friend and still a role model of mine). Joe took one look at our business and said:

"Guys, you need to hire an acquisition manager!"

At first, we were resistant to his advice. We couldn't really say why, it had something to do with relinquishing control over that part of our business. I mean, getting contracts signed was the most important part. Why did he think we should find some new person and let *them* do it?

Despite our resistance, we decided to give it a shot. At the time, we didn't have any idea of the impact it would have. We just saw it as a somewhat risky move that might end up working out. We ran our job ads, found a few candidates, did the interviews, and hired one. Nothing fancy.

We actually ended up with a great sales rep. I honestly think we got lucky. I wrote this book so that you won't have to rely on luck to end up with a rockstar sales rep like we did.

We didn't really train our AM. We went on a couple appointments with him and then just threw him to the wolves. Now he was officially in-between us and all of the sellers.

Every time a call came in, we had someone who answered it, went to their house, ran numbers, made offers, and brought back contracts. He also made ALL the follow up calls to the sellers that didn't turn into contracts.

(BTW, our average "contact to contract" timeframe is 60+ days. This means that, on average, it takes 2 months from the time a lead comes in for it to become a contract. Still think you don't need someone to help you with follow up?)

Customers will call, email, and text all hours of the day, and on weekends. You're out to dinner with your wife (or husband), and the phone is blowing up. You're on an appointment with a seller who is giving you an earful about their life, and you're thinking about your ever-growing to-do list that waits for you when you get home. Having an AM assures that this will never happen to you again. They protect you from all of that communication because they are doing it themselves. You only hear about the important details, like "Hey, I got 2 contracts signed today!"

Nowadays, I understand that all of the above is *supposed* to happen when you hire the right person to replace you in any area of your business. But since that was our first time experiencing it, it felt like **magic.**

Once our AM had been up and running for a few months, we started to see a lot more contracts rolling in. We also had a lot more time on our hands. We were able to use that time strategizing how to grow the business. We spent a lot of time on marketing, driving as many leads as we could to our AM. We were still doing a lot of stuff we shouldn't have been, like all the "office manager" type stuff. But, things were really looking up.

Since then, we've been fortunate enough to replace ourselves in nearly every area of our business. Yet, I still look back at the AM as the most important and beneficial replacement we've ever made.

THE BIGGEST PITFALL FOR NEWBIES
When I coach my clients, I discover that their two biggest problems are:

- Not doing enough marketing to generate leads, and/or
- Not answering the calls that come in, going on appointments, making offers, or following up!

The above activities are at the **core** of any successful real estate business. If these things aren't getting done, you won't make money. The one who has the contracts has the gold. Always remember that.

If the above items are getting done, you will make money, but you will still be busy as hell. That's why you hire people and start to replace yourself.

Here's the problem: You are either 1) too scared to do the above, or 2) too strapped for time to do it. Or maybe you aren't scared but you genuinely dislike being a salesperson, it's just not one of your strengths.

Trust me, I understand where you're coming from. I'm here with good news...you don't have to be your company's sales rep. In fact...you shouldn't be! There are more qualified people out there that will do a better job than you. That's great news, isn't it?

Make sure you heard me: If you do not want to talk to sellers, go on appointments, get contracts signed, and follow up, you don't have to. But, you DO have to hire the right person to do it for you.

You need to be taking the calls live, scheduling appointments with **anyone** who will agree to it, attending those appointments, following a proven sales process to convert, making offers, and following up frequently. You absolutely have to do those things if you want to get deals in this real estate market.

Nothing on the MLS is a very good deal for an investor, and realtors usually spoonfeed the best pocket listings to the big developers in your area.

That's why we have to become **marketing and sales organizations at heart.** We don't want the stuff that everyone else is competing for. We want to buy at a discount. Hiring your first sales rep is a giant stride towards doing that.

Even if you are awesome at sales and want to do it yourself, there's still a really big problem with that. Someone has to drive leads to the AM to keep them busy. Marketing is a full time job in itself. If you can't afford to hire someone to do that too, then it's your responsibility.

What about managing the renovations once you buy these properties? Managing finances? Building your rental portfolio? Operations? Being a leader, visionary, CEO? Getting coaching/mentorship? Learning? Building a healthy culture for your team? Focusing on creating a better experience for your customer?

Are you going to sacrifice all of those aspects of your company so that you can cling to the role of rockstar sales rep? Do you really think you can build a large, successful company that way? A **real** business?

Another variable to consider is this: Even if you are twice as good as the rep you could hire, I bet you aren't going on appointments all week long. A good rep should attend 10-12 appointments every week, no matter what (explained more in Chapter 4). That's 2-3 per day!

Appointments can be 2 hours long sometimes, and they can also be an hour drive away. Plus you have to prepare for these appointments too (run comps, etc). Then you usually have to follow up. The role of an AM, when done properly, is a 40 hour work week, easy.

You can't beat a guy who is going on 12 appointments per week and following up diligently if you're only going on 2-3 and not following up like you should. Your rep, even if they are only 60% as good as you at sales, will outperform you 3 to 1 simply due to the sheer volume of activity they are generating.

The best part about hiring an AM is that it creates so much time that you can apply towards growing the business. Ever read "The E-Myth Revisited" by Michael Gerber? Do you remember what his MAIN advice in that book is?

"Go to work ON your business rather than IN it".

- *Michael Gerber*

The business owner should spend as much time as possible working ON the business and as little time as possible working IN the business. That's how a business develops. That's how you can grow to 7 figures in revenue and have a team that does EVERY part of the job FOR YOU. That's how you create a business that is automated, one that generates income for you whether you work or not. Is that something you want?

If you've never hired an Acquisition Manager (or any employee) before, then this is a perfect opportunity to learn and grow. This book you hold in your hands gives you everything you need to stop merely reading about Gerber's advice and start applying it.

One AM won't run your whole business for you. But aside from the benefits I've already described, there's one more. Making this hire will change your **mindset.** You'll shift from being less "self-employed" to more "business owner". Once you learn how powerful it is to leverage other people, and how to do it, you'll NEVER want to go back to doing the work yourself. And if you do it correctly, **you'll never have to.**

HOW TO EXAMINE AND ELIMINATE YOUR FEARS

The resistance I had towards making my first hire was strong. It's likely that you are experiencing the very same thing. Please be aware of that resistance when it pops up. You probably had some resistance to this idea from the moment you read the title of the book. That's normal. If this applies to you, you need to examine that resistance more deeply before you move forward. Otherwise you won't.

I'm serious. Write down the answer to these questions before reading any further. It won't take that long.

———

EXAMINE AND ELIMINATE YOUR FEARS - QUESTIONS

Describe the feeling of resistance you have towards hiring an AM in more detail:

Why do you feel this way?

What are you most worried about?

What benefit could hiring an AM have on your revenue?

What benefit could hiring an AM have on your free time?

If you hired an AM and it went bad, what does the worst case scenario look like?

What would you do to get out of that scenario?

On a scale of 1-10, how BAD would you rate your worst case scenario?

I got the idea of examining your "worst case scenario" from Tim Ferriss. Basically, you're analyzing your fears. If you're ever scared to take action and that fear paralyzed you from moving forward, the least you can do is take some time to analyze what's going on.

Don't take your fear at "face value". Fear/worry/anxiety all feel like shit to experience. They really do. But a lot of the time, the fears are imagined. They're made up. They're not rational or logical. Examining them can go a long way towards getting rid of them.

Chapter 2
HOW TO FIND THE CANDIDATES

THE BEST AM JOB POSTING IN THE WORLD
The first step towards hiring your first AM is to create a badass job posting. We post our ads on Craigslist and Indeed. We post the ads weekly, in both the "real estate" and "sales" sections.

Below is a the exact ad we use. The content of this ad will make more sense when you read the "Automated Hiring Funnel" section afterwards.

———

Acquisition Manager Sample Job Posting

Work From Home - Set Your Own Hours - Make 50K+++
(Your Company) is looking to hire and train a hungry, self-motivated outside sales person to join our company.

At (Your Company), you can:

Make 50K ++ your first year
Work from home/coffee shops/wherever
Set your own hours
Be part of a energized, hungry, growing team
Join our book club
Go out for beers with the team after a productive week
Go on snowboarding trips with the team
Be coached towards developing yourself personally, profes-
sionally, and financially
Be your own entrepreneur within our business
Feel like you have a sense of ownership
Get amazing sales training
Make some damn good friends

At (Your Company), you will:

Call sellers about their properties
Negotiate
Overcome Objections
Go on appointments
Get contracts
Be challenged to reach your goals
Be challenged to grow and think outside the box
Be asked for your opinion on how the business can grow

At (Your Company), you must:

Be a team player
Be a self starter

Be the kind of person we'd want to hang out with
Be willing to learn
Be willing to examine your strengths and weaknesses
Be committed to the growth of yourself and the company

If we sound like a good fit for you, please follow the directions below - explicitly! Candidates who don't complete **all three steps** will **not** be considered.

1) Reply to this posting with your resume attached.
2) Complete this survey (copy and paste into browser): www. yoursurveymonkeylink.com
3) Make a video of yourself (No longer than 5 minutes) telling us a little about you and why you think you are a good fit for the job. Post the video on Youtube or elsewhere and send us a link to it. If you use YouTube, make sure the video is "unlisted" or "public" so that we can see it. We won't be able to watch a video marked "private".

Thanks!
Your Company Name
www.yourcompanywebsite.com

Note: All candidates are required to pass a background check before being hired.

———

Yes, we mention beer and snowboarding in our ad. Don't be afraid to show your personality/company culture in your job postings. You'll attract the right people and repel the wrong ones. If you think this whole process has to be all stuffy, formal, and corporate, you've got it all wrong.

(By the way, you have my permission to use this ad for your job posting. Just remember to tweak it to fit your company.)

In the job posting, you don't need to reveal the exact pay structure you will offer (I discuss how to pay your AM in the next chapter). Just come up with an estimate of about how much they can expect to make and add "+++", assuming they will be a rockstar and blow your expectations out of the water.

For example, if your business does 500K per year and you plan on paying them around 10% commission, you'd say "50K+++". You assume that, when they come into your business, they are going to dramatically increase your revenue.

BUILD YOUR AUTOMATED HIRING FUNNEL

What I'm about to share will save you TONS of time when hiring your first AM. You can expect to get 50-100 applicants from a well-written job posting. That's a LOT. You don't want to look through all those resumes. Nor will they tell you that much. That's why your job posting contains a "funnel". Like the sample job post above, your job post should ask applicants to complete the following steps:

Step 1: Reply to the job posting by email with their resume attached.

You want them to do this but you don't need to read any of the resumes yet. In fact, you'll look at only a few of them, later.

TIP: Create a separate email address for the job posting replies to go to so these emails don't mix with your personal or work email. There's way too many of them and it's much cleaner to keep it separate.

Step 2: Click on the link provided and fill out the survey (through Survey Monkey).

You'll need to create this survey inside Survey Monkey and then post a link to it in your job ad. Come up with 5 to 10 questions that you'd like them to answer. The survey questions aren't super important at this stage but they can be helpful. The larger purpose of the survey (and this funnel) is to find out if they are serious about the job and if they can follow directions.

Step 3: Record a short video (5 minutes or less) introducing themselves and explaining why they think they would be a good fit for the job.

This is the secret: out of every 100 applicants, only 3-5 of them will actually send in videos. The job posting clearly states that you have to complete all 3 steps to be considered, but 95% of applicants didn't read that far down, or ignored it. So now you get to ignore them.

So, instead of combing through 100 boring resumes, you get to watch 3-5 short videos where you can actually see and hear the people you might be hiring. You can then go into your email and review the resumes for ONLY those that submitted videos. All those other resumes? Forget about them. Those people can't follow instructions.

I love the videos because I operate largely on intuition and I believe I can get a good feel for someone's attitude, energy, personality, and motivation when I watch their video. Sometimes I know within 30 seconds whether or not someone is going to be a good fit.

I still remember the video our current Marketing Director sent in. He had one of those large paper easels and he had drawn diagrams and pictures that illustrated his life. He passionately went through each "slide" he had created on the easel over the course of his 5 minute video. He came across as likable, engaging, and intelligent. Do you think he stood out, just a tad, from all those other losers who just sent me an email saying "resume attached"?

So, if I need to hire a new sales rep, here's what the process looks like:

1) Ask the office manager to post the ad
2) Wait a couple weeks, receive around 5 videos
3) Watch the videos & schedule 3-4 phone interviews
4) Conduct phone interviews
5) Schedule 2-3 in-person interviews
6) Hire someone (if I find the right person)

Bottom Line: The funnel is a beautiful way to skip RIGHT to the people who are more likely to be a good fit for this role.

Chapter 3
HOW TO INTERVIEW THE CANDIDATES

HOW TO PAY YOUR AM

I included this section right here because I'm sure it's on your mind and you're going to need to tell the applicants what the pay structure looks like during the interview anyways.

I've seen probably a hundred real estate investing businesses at this point. The way they pay their acquisition managers varies. What I'll give you here is what we do, and what I think the industry average is.

Most businesses pay their acquisition managers somewhere from 8-20% commission on the gross profit. That means if you grossed 30K profit on a flip, and the AM was paid 10% commission, he or she would take home $3,000. To tighten up that range a bit, I'd say 10-15% is probably the sweet spot. How much you want to give is up to you.

You can also play with the idea of paying them a flat fee per deal, plus bonuses if they are able to negotiate deep discounts on the properties. For example, you could pay your AM $1,000 per closed deal plus an additional $500 for every 10K they negotiate off of your MAO (Max Allowable Offer). So if you send them on the appointment saying "The most we can pay for this is 70K" and they bring it back for 50K, they just earned an extra $1,000.

In our company, we've paid AM's anywhere from 8-15%. It varies and changes over time. We increase their percentage a couple points if they have to do the Transaction Coordination (more on that in Chapter 7), because that's more work for them and it saves us $$ by not having to pay someone else to do it.

One mistake we made in the past was starting too high in the beginning. We offered our first AM 15%. Later, we really needed to move him down to 10% to make our numbers work. That was an awkward conversation. I can tell you that it's much easier to go UP than it is to go down. Start low and you can increase their pay later. Follow the principle of *underpromise and overdeliver.*

Another important variable is **draw.** If you don't know what draw is, it's money you pay an employee that they have to pay you back out of their future commissions. Many commission-only sales jobs come with draw for the first 30-90 days. This is because it takes a while for sales reps to get deals in the pipeline and start earning commissions.

For example, you might decide to pay your AM $400 in draw per week for the first 60 days. By the end of that, they're going to owe you $3,200, if no closings have taken place during that time (that they generated). If a deal closes the following month that the AM was set to make $2,500 on, they will make nothing, and the draw owed will be reduced to $700. Sometimes we only make our AM apply a portion of their commission to paying back the draw, so they can at least keep some of it. You can structure it however you want.

One important thing to not screw up: don't ever pay any employee draw for more than 90 days. Commissioned employees must earn their keep. If you pay draw for too long you take the pressure off them to earn. If your AM isn't filling the pipeline within 90 days, there's a bigger problem somewhere and you've got to find it.

Sometimes, you may lose an employee who still owes you draw. They could either quit or get fired. In these cases, I simply write off the loss and move on. I don't think it's reasonable to expect them to pay me back. This is another reason to cap the period during which an employee can receive draw (to 90 days or less). It limits your exposure.

Ultimately, run your numbers and come up with the best pay structure for your situation. Settle on something you feel comfortable with and good about.

Some of you are cringing at the thought of giving up 10% of your profit to someone else.

Consider this:

Let's say your RE business is doing 400K per year, with an average deal size of 20K. That's 20 deals a year. If your AM came to work for you (at 10% commission) and didn't increase your revenue at all (which would be an epic failure), he'd take 40K of your revenue and you'd keep 360K. If he only brought in a mere 2 extra deals beyond what you were already bringing in over the **entire year**, you'd be a 440K, or 396,000 after you paid him his 44K commission. That's almost exactly where you were before you hired the AM. So 2 extra deals per year would be the "break even" point in this scenario. Anything beyond that is more money than you would have made.

Plus, you wouldn't keep a guy around unless he was dramatically improving your situation, not just bringing in a couple extra deals per year. In addition to that, we've not even factored in the massive amount of time you've gotten back to focus on marketing and other things (like getting your sanity back).

HOW TO EXECUTE THE PHONE INTERVIEWS

OK, so you've gotten a handful of videos and scheduled some phone interviews with your favorite candidates. Here's what to do next.

Step one is to conduct a short (20 minute maximum) phone interview with the candidates whose videos you liked. At this stage you're really just determining whether they are worth a longer in-person interview. If you are on the fence about an applicant (who, of course, sent in a video), go ahead and schedule them for a phone interview. Sometimes people will surprise you. Plus, you'll get better at this everytime you do it. It's good practice. It gives the applicant some interview practice of their own, which is never a bad thing.

THE BEST PHONE INTERVIEW QUESTIONS

Here are some great questions to ask during the phone interview:

———

Phone Interview Questions
Tell me about yourself?
What are your most important values?
What kind of things will you not compromise on? (Looking for more about their values)
What are your goals for the next 6 to 12 months?
What kind of job do you see yourself holding 3 to 5 years from now?
What things frustrate you the most? How do you usually cope?
What makes you unique? Why should I hire you over these other people?
What is it about this job that you are most interested in and why?

Are you currently employed?

Do you have any sales experience? (If yes, please explain. If no, why do you feel that you are a good fit?)

What did you like least about your last job? What did you like most?

What's your current availability?

What books are you reading?

What do you love to learn?

Why are you leaving your job?

Full disclosure of their job responsibilities and the challenges, are they 100% ok with them?

What's a weakness that you have?

If you're offered the job, what will you require from us in order to accept it?

How much money do you have to make for this to work?

How much money do you really want to make within the next 12 months?

What questions do you have for us?

(At the end, you're looking for someone who "closes" the interview like you'd close a sale. If your candidate can't close you, or doesn't even try, how do you expect them to do it in the field with customers?)

———

Remember that you may need to interview 4-8 people over the phone in order to end up with about 2-3 solid in-person interview candidates. I would not recommend making a hiring decision without interviewing at least 3 people in-person. Even if you really like one of them, you need other people to **compare** them to. It gives you some contrast and prevents you from falling in love with one candidate and ignoring the rest.

First impressions aren't everything. Some people are great at interviewing but not so great at working. That's why the due diligence for this hire is so extensive. We're going to make sure you end up with the best AM possible.

WHAT TO LOOK FOR IN YOUR AM

You're looking for quite a few things.

First off, you're looking for a closer. Someone who asks you things like:

"What's it going to take for me to land this job?
"Have I not done enough to prove to you that I'm the right person?"
"What do you need to see from me for me to get hired?"
"How can I prove to you that I'm the right person?"
"When can I expect to hear a decision from you?"

You're also looking for someone who can listen. If your candidate can't pay attention, interrupts, or comes off as abrasive, he's going to do that to the customer, too. You might have experience with aggressive, pushy salespeople and think that those traits are desirable, or necessary to close deals. They're not.

Being pushy and aggressive is a fall back strategy for sales reps who don't have the right training, or the right personalities for the job. The best sales reps are calm. The best reps sell by asking questions and listening. They are definitely dominant and assertive, but only at the right times. Later in this chapter, I'll go into more detail on the traits you *must have* in your AM.

I prefer hiring candidates in the age range of 25-35. I didn't start by actively seeking out people of any particular age. I ended up with nothing but young(er) hires and then dissected why that was happening. Here's what I found:

Someone fresh out of college is hungry to enter the workforce and grow their careers. They often haven't made a lot of money yet and are motivated by the potential for high earnings in my company. They are also more capable of and willing to live off a small draw (or nothing at all) until the commissions start rolling in. Younger, out-of-college applicants don't usually have big houses and expensive cars (or habits).

This is important for you because you don't want very much upfront cost associated with this hire. You only want to pay them when YOU get paid, via commission. You want to hire them when your company is still young (6 figures in yearly revenue), because they will help the company grow rapidly by exploding sales.

But, until that happens, they need to be OK making 50-80K a year or whatever it ends up being. Younger candidates tend to be more OK with that. In fact, they're ecstatic about it because it's the most money they've ever made, and they get to make it working for you out in the field versus inside some stuffy cubicle.

Also, younger candidates are usually more coachable and trainable if they don't come with a decade of experience under their belt. The last thing you want is someone who won't listen to your suggestions and isn't interested in growing their skills and admitting their faults. That doesn't have to do with age, but with experience.

Am I saying that you **don't** want someone with sales experience? Not exactly. But a lot of sales training is crappy. Once hired, you're going to give your AM the best sales training there is. Plus,

BRIAN ELLWOOD

in our company, personal growth and development is our core value. So for us, it's extremely important that new team members come with an open mind, ready to be shaped and molded into their highest selves.

You want someone with a high energy level. I like for my applicants to be in shape, workout regularly, and possibly have a sports background (makes them competitive). I like for them to have very organized personal lives. Someone who wakes up and goes to bed at the same time, works out certain days of the week, lives by their calendar, doesn't "drop the ball" on things, etc. They shouldn't come across as "lazy" in any way. They should have active lives, both during the week and on weekends. Very important stuff.

You don't want to hire someone who is too off-putting. I've heard some investors say they won't hire an AM if he has a big beard. I personally have a beard and am a big fan of beards, but I understand what they're saying. Most customers don't have beards, so they could have trouble relating to your AM if he does.

People like others who look, dress, and act like **they** do. Every little bit helps. Picture each of your AM candidates sitting in the living room with the customer. How will your customer relate to them? Will they be able to?

Hint: If you can't have a bearded sales rep, at least require every man in your company to have a beard. It gives you strength! :)

Back to the age thing: There are plenty of applicants of all ages who fit the above criteria. In my own experience, folks in their 20's and 30's **more often** fit the above criteria. But, you can/ should hire at any age, as along as the candidate fits what you are looking for.

26

Lastly, you're looking for someone who shares your own values. For me, personal development is at my core. I don't really vibe well with people who aren't interested in learning new things, picking up a book, setting and achieving goals, etc. It's not that there's anything wrong with those people, but I personally don't **enjoy** working alongside them. So I make sure that everyone I hire is big into their personal growth.

You need to decide what values are important to **you** and look for those in your candidates. No one is more qualified than you to make someone a part of your business. Sales does require unique skills, but it is no exception. Always put values **first.**

Note: The above statement, like many sections of this book, should be applied to ALL hires within your business, not just the AM.

HOW TO CONDUCT THE IN-PERSON INTERVIEWS

By now you should have chosen your 3 candidates for the in-person interviews. The in-person interviews are a lot more thorough and in depth.

If you don't have an office, meet your candidates in the lobby of a nice hotel. It gives off an air of professionalism and is a nice way to meet in public. Just make sure the lobby has appropriate seating and is relatively quiet. I schedule all my in-person interviews back-to-back on the same day. I dress nice for the interviews but I keep the vibe pretty laid back. You need to find out if you're going to connect with this person and enjoy being around them. You can't find that out unless you **be yourself** at all times.

Anyone who is part of the hiring decision should be in attendance. If you have a small team, it wouldn't hurt to bring everyone to these interviews. Making sure your new hire is a good culture fit is just as important as their sales skills.

As a side note, I always ask my team members to go out for a beer with a candidate when I'm on the brink of hiring them. The team always give me great feedback, things I didn't notice myself. If the team doesn't click with the candidate, it foreshadows future problems. I don't hire that person and keep on looking.

The in-person interviews usually take 30-60 minutes. The ones that only last 30 minutes are usually a sign that the candidate wasn't a good fit. If you get a candidate that really interests you, you aren't going to want to let them leave. You'll keep finding questions to ask, or relatable things to talk about. Those interviews go over an hour and that can be a good sign.

But, don't let anything too unrelated distract you from making a disciplined decision. Below are the questions we use for the in-person interviews. These questions are kind of "tough", so you might even want to practice asking them ahead of time, on anyone who's willing.

THE BEST IN-PERSON INTERVIEW QUESTIONS

Finding out how committed your AM candidate is:
Tell me about a major struggle in your past and how you overcame it?
What changes did you need to make to overcome it?

Finding out if your AM candidate has/thrives off having goals:
What are your top 3 life goals? Why did you choose those goals?
How are you doing in terms of achieving those goals?
What kinds of accomplishments are most gratifying to you?

<u>Finding out if your AM Candidate really has sales experience:</u>
The job posting mentioned that you need to be __. How do you know you have those traits?
How do I know that's true?

<u>Finding out how seasoned your AM candidate is:</u>
Why does anyone choose to "buy" a product or service?
What steps do you think are included in selling a product?
How long does it take for you to close a sale?
Describe a typical day for you.
How do you plan your day? How do you manage your time? Why is it important to do it that way?
How much time do you spend doing activities other than selling, like paperwork and data collection?
What kind of people do you like to work with?
What do you dislike about sales?

<u>Finding out if your AM candidate is competitive:</u>
Tell me about a time when you had to reach a goal in only a short period of time, and what you did to make that happen.
In your last sales job, how did you rank compared to the rest of the sales reps? (If they didn't have a sales job, how did they rank compared to the rest of the employees?)

<u>Finding out how decisive your AM candidate is:</u>
If I offered you the job today, would you be able to give me a firm yes or no, assuming I tell you everything you need to know about the job?
What was your last major purchase? How did you decide to buy? Why that way?

Finding out if your AM candidate is resilient:
How do you handle objections?
Tell me about a time when a sale really went bad. What did you do to pick up the pieces?
Describe your most devastating failure.
Describe a specific time you were rejected. How did you handle that?
When you don't meet your sales goals, how does that make you feel?
What do you do to correct it?
How smart are you, in comparison to your friends?

Finding out your AM candidate's feelings and expectations about their income:
What was the most money you ever made inside of one year? What year was that?
How much money did you make last year?
How much do you expect to make this year?
How much do you earn in an average year?
How comfortable are you making that amount? Is that enough for you?

Finding out if your AM candidate will be proactive in generating their own leads:
How do you plan to generate leads on your own?
Aren't there any better ways than that?
What else would you do?
Anything else? (Look for creativity)
What skills do you think are needed to be successful in sales over the phone?

What roadblocks do you expect when trying to build rapport with a customer in the beginning? How do you respond?

What will you do in the first 30 days if I were to hire you? 60 days? 90 days?

Finding out if your AM can close:

How do I know you could close a sale?

I'm still not convinced.

I'm STILL not convinced.

Do you have any questions for me? (Look for a closer. Your AM candidate should be very curious about whether or not they are going to get the job, and what is going to happen next.)

———

That last statement "I'm still not convinced" is **really** important. No matter WHAT they say, you have to say it. Twice. You can tell them what you were up to later on if it makes you feel better. But you need to see how they react under that type of pressure.

"Convince me" is a tricky spot to be in. It's like in the sales movies when they hand they guy a ballpoint pen and say "Sell me that pen". Pressure's on. They'll be under pressure every day if they come to work for you. You need to see how they handle it. If they fold and say "well, I guess I can't convince you", then they just saved you a lot of trouble, because you know you shouldn't hire them.

You don't need to ask every question in the list above. Select the ones that you like the most and make your own list of questions. Add other questions to it. Feel good about it. But don't be too soft, you need to put some pressure on someone who is interviewing for an AM position. It's part of the job.

THE CONTEST THAT WILL TELL YOU THE TRUTH

Once the in-person interviews have been completed, there's one more step you need to do. You're going to initiate a "contest" between the top 1-3 candidates. Even if you only have 1 candidate you're interested in, have them complete this contest anyways.

If you have leads already, divide them up and provide the candidate(s) with them. They should be given no more than 1 week (Monday - Friday) to call as many of them as possible, find out the seller's motivation (their "why" for selling), asking price, and if they are willing to receive a written offer from your company. If you want, you can have them schedule appointments too, but you'll have to go on them yourself if you don't have an AM already.

The above sequence isn't the best way to handle your leads. You can alter it however you want. Getting deals is not the point here. You're seeing how these AM's will work if hired.

If you don't want to give them your leads to work, or you don't have any leads, simply have them call properties listed for sale on Zillow, Craigslist, the MLS, FSBO sites, etc. You're trying to find out how quickly and intelligently they work, and if they can sell. How hard do they try? Are they trying to find deals, or just going through the motions? Do they send you an email every 5 minutes asking questions, or do they figure stuff out on their own? Are they comfortable moving forward without having all the answers?

At the end of the week, there will almost always be a clear winner. Sometimes, the person we liked the most will quit by Tuesday! Good thing we did the contest before we hired them. That is why it's critical that you don't skip this step. What someone tells you versus how they actually work can be very different.

If you feel bad about asking your candidates to do so much crap before being hired, I understand. You can offer to pay them (a little bit) to complete the contest portion. But, I almost hesitate to suggest that because you really want someone who's committed to getting this job at all costs. There is a line that you can cross, though, where you're asking too much. At the end of the day offering them $100-200 to complete this challenge isn't going to screw up your results that much.

THE KOLBE & DISC TESTS

The Kolbe and DISC tests are both very popular, widely used personality tests. You must have your AM take one, or both, of these. You can have them do this during the same time they are completing the "contest" described above.

With the DISC test, You are looking for people who score high in the "D" (Dominant) and "I" (Influence) categories. Someone with this profile will be able to maintain control of the situation when on appointments, which is critical if they are going to follow a sales process and not get sidetracked.

At the time of this writing, Tony Robbins has a free DISC test available on his website, here:

https://www.tonyrobbins.com/disc/

The Kolbe test is a fantastic test for learning more about someone's personality. We tested everyone inside of our business on it. I think it costs about $50 per person. I'd only recommend testing 1-2 potential hires with this, since it isn't free.

What you're looking for in the Kolbe results of an AM is a **high quick start.** That quick start trait is **crucial** to a salesperson's success. Don't hire anyone who isn't at least a **6 or higher** on the quick start scale.

A high quick start is someone who takes action without knowing all the details first. You want a rep who is chomping at the bit to get in front of customers, not one who is at home overanalyzing everything and too afraid to move forward.

Hint: A lot of entrepreneurs have high quick start personalities. If you are the type that takes massive action without knowing all of the facts, this probably describes you. It's a great trait for a salesperson. The fact that you are high quick start is probably part of the reason that you don't want to relinquish the job of being your company's sales rep. You don't think they will go as hard as you do. That's why you need to make sure to hire someone **like you!**

THE BACKGROUND CHECK

Once you've made your hiring decision, you need to get a background check done on all team members. I learned this lesson the hard way. A guy we hired conned us out of $15,000 (this wasn't a sales rep but another position). We later found out that he was a multiple felon, convicted of identity theft and fraud. Spend the $50 to make sure you aren't about to hire someone like him. Your job ad, like the sample one in this book, should clearly state that all applicants must pass a background check. This should keep some of the wolves at bay.

THE NONCOMPETE CONTRACT

A noncompete is a contract that prevents one of your employees from taking all of your strategies, leaving your company and starting their own company that competes with yours, using all of your techniques. They can do all of that eventually, but the noncompete sets the time frame during which they are not allowed.

Most noncompetes range from 1-10 years. Find a noncompete online and adjust the wording to your liking. You can also have your attorney draft this.

What we do is make our sales rep sign a noncompete agreeing that he/she will not conduct business similar to ours, in our geographic region, for 2 full years upon employment termination.

This prevents someone from coming in, learning our business model, quitting, and immediately copying our business model in our own backyard, thus becoming a source of competition.

It's common in many industries to get these signed by new employees. You can adjust the above terms in any way that suits you. Don't feel bad about asking for this. Anyone who doesn't have a hidden agenda will have no problem signing it.

Chapter 4
HOW TO ONBOARD, TRAIN, AND MANAGE YOUR NEW AM

EVERYTHING YOU NEED TO GET YOUR AM GOING
Once your candidate has formally accepted the position, signed the noncompete, and completed the background check, you're ready to rock and roll. Pick a date for them to start. Block out an entire week to train them and bring them up to speed on how your business works.

Here's a list of the most common items you'll need to go over with your new AM:

1) **Phone System** - We use Talkdesk and link our AM's cell phone to it so we can track how many work calls they make (versus personal calls). That is a KPI we track. You could start out with something as simple as a Google Voice number for them, and upgrade to a more robust phone service provider later.

2) **CRM** - Get them set up with whatever CRM you use (the place where you store all your leads). I highly recommend

using Podio for this. You can build an "app" very easily that will store all of your leads. You can automate a lot of actions straight from Podio, as well as set up obvious things like a status/buckets for leads to go in, next follow up dates/ reminders, etc. Watch some videos on Podio. The possibilities are endless with it. Many high level investors not only keep all their leads in Podio, but they also run their entire businesses within it. If you want something super simple, you can keep leads on a Google spreadsheet starting out. But you'll need to graduate from that fairly soon after.

3) **Email account** - Your AM will need a work email address, one that you maintain control over. Remember, the relationships that they build with customers are owned by **you,** not them. You paid for the marketing to generate those relationships. In the event that you have to let them go, you need to take back the email account as well. Start a free Google business account where you can create email addresses with your company name in them. For example: Chris@tampahousebuyers.com

4) **Slack** - I highly recommend all small businesses use Slack as their primary means of internal communication. It's much easier than emailing. Try it. Watch some instructional videos on how to use it. You'll see what I mean! It improves communication between your team members and cuts down on emails. It's also much easier to search and upload attachments than doing it within your email. We use Slack for all of our calls with one another, it has a cool video/webcam call feature so we can see each other when we're working together.

5) **Voxer** - Use this to communicate with your rep on the fly. It's like a Walkie Talkie for your phone. Much faster and less

cumbersome than texting. Also cuts down on long emails/ Slack messages. I use Voxer with my coaching students so that we don't have to write novels to one another via email.

6) **"Wearable" microphone** - I recommend finding a microphone that either works with their cellphone, or something that can be put in their pocket or around their neck. These are used to record the conversation that happens during the appointments. These recordings are very valuable towards knowing how your AM is performing in the field. You'll need these recordings if you want to hold your AM accountable to following the sales process, explained in Chapter 5. We use microphones that look like flash drives that the reps wear around their neck. You may need to get permission from the customer to record the appointment. The recording is for educational purposes but, if you don't explain that and get permission, you could make some people uncomfortable.

7) **Company T-Shirt** - get your AM at least 2-3 company t-shirts. You can go button up, collared, or both. Company logo sewn on. If you don't have a logo get someone on Fiverr to make you one easily. These shirts give off a professional appearance. It's a couple hundred bucks that you'll easily get back.

8) **Sales Training** - You need to acquire sales training for your rep. I go into more detail on sales training later in this chapter. If you don't have much money for this, pick out a great sales book that you and your rep will read together and pick things to implement. "Never Split the Difference" is a great book to start with.

9) **Repair Education** - I recommend setting your AM up with some training on how to identify defects in a house. As you'll

see in the next section, you'll be using your AM to run repair estimates for you. If you don't know how to do this yourself, you need to find someone or a program that can educate both you and your AM. Taking a home inspection certification course will go a long way to understanding the components of a house and what things look like when they're broken. Most cities have regular Home Inspection Certification classes. They should only last a week and will provide you with a lifetime of value. (more on this in Chapter 8)

HOW TO BE A GREAT SALES MANAGER

So you're not the AM anymore...congrats! You have a ton of your time back. How should you spend it? Can you just kick your feet up and expect results?

Hell no!

You now have a new role. You are your company's "Sales Manager". Even if you only have one rep to manage. You must give yourself that title, officially and publicly to the company.

As the Sales Manager, it is your responsibility to:

1) Talk with your AM a minimum of one hour per week
2) Dig deep into the "why" of the AM. Really learn what they want out of this job and, more importantly, out of life. Help them decide on their own how the AM role is linked to their larger goals.
3) Go over key KPI's with your AM (broken down in the next section). Find out what needs to be done and create a plan to improve them
4) Create and review your Sales Process
5) Hold AM accountable to following all steps in the Sales Process

6) Review call recordings and appointment recordings
7) Discuss anything that's bothering your AM
8) Go over things learned in sales training
9) Continue to learn about becoming a better manager and a better leader, which is critical if you want to build a real business.

KPI'S TO WATCH LIKE A HAWK

Key Performance Indicators (KPI's) live at the heart of any successful business. You have to know what numbers are important, and look at them all the time. You must set goals for your KPI's and always be strategizing on how you will hit those goals.

Here are the main KPI's that we track and hold our AM accountable to:

1) **Outbound Calls** - Tie your AM's phone to your phone service provider and track how many outbound calls they make. They should be able to make 50-100 calls per week, even with a full appointment schedule. If they aren't able to schedule/attend a single appointment, it's reasonable to expect them to make 300+ calls that week. I know that sounds like a lot, but if your AM won't do it, another one will.

2) **Appointments Attended** - How many times did your AM visit a seller at their home? 10-12 per week is the sweet spot (I explain why later in this chapter). If you have a lot of appointments getting cancelled, examine the process you have in place that leads up to the appointment. See if you can add in Advance Agreements (discussed in Chapter 5) or set expectations more clearly. Also, set more appointments than you want to go on, because a handful will always fall through.

3) **Offers Made** - This refers to how many written offers your AM sent out each week. This could happen in person, via mail, or email. We let our AM's track this themselves and report their number back to us.

4) **Contracts Signed** - We expect our AM's to bring back at least 2 contracts per week. It's different in every business depending on whether you are a wholesaler, rehabber, builder, the competitiveness of your market, your average deal size, etc. You may or may not need that many contracts. But, this is the ultimate KPI for your AM. All the other KPI's *lead* to this one.

If an AM is going on appointments, making offers, and not bringing back any contracts, they better have a really good and believable reason why, otherwise it's time to let them go.

HIGH APPOINTMENTS IS THE WAY

Here's a tip you're going to love. I was taught this by Sean Terry, a successful investor and podcaster who is part of my mastermind group. As soon as he revealed it, everyone in the mastermind group started doing it and their businesses took off!

As I said above, one of the KPI's you must track with your AM is appointments attended per week. This is critical. If your AM isn't meeting with sellers and making offers all week long, then they aren't doing their job.

We used to allow our AM's to sit back and wait for a "lay down" deal. They wouldn't go on the appointment unless they were pretty sure they were going to get the contract signed. They'd wait until someone agreed to the price over the phone, and basically go to the house just to pick up the contract. This is very bad practice and it won't result in a lot of deals.

Before a seller meets you, they have no idea who you are. You're just someone who sent them something in the mail, and they talked to you on the phone. When you meet them in person, it's a game changer. They get a sense of whether or not they can trust you. If you can establish trust, they will open up to you and start to tell you the real reasons why they are selling.

You wouldn't believe how often a seller will dramatically reduce their price once they meet you in person. Their walls come down. We've seen multiple scenarios where a seller will come down from 200K to 100K during the appointment. They probably knew they would come down all along, but they weren't willing to admit that over the phone (show their cards). This is why it's critical to get in front of sellers. Most of your competitors will hear that 200K, say "nope", and move onto the next lead.

Of course, if you already have a full schedule of 12 appointments for that week, and someone wants twice what the property is worth, you wouldn't attend that appointment. The point here is that if you haven't hit the 12 appointment goal, **set and attend any appointment possible.**

For one, it's really good practice for your AM - they get to go through the Sales Process another time, make offers, handle rejections, develop their people skills, etc. The more comfortable they get, the more contracts they'll bring back. Don't let your AM hang around at a coffee shop waiting on the easy deals. Hold them accountable to going on 10-12 appointments per week. You'll thank me later for this tip.

I recently looked back at several **years** worth of our KPI's. I was only looking at two columns, appointments attended and contracts signed. Almost like clockwork, anytime the AM went on 10 or more appointments that week, he brought back 3 or more signed contracts. During weeks when he went on 5 appointments, he got 0-1 signed contracts. There's a "carry over" effect too - if you go on 12 appointments one week you might only get 2 deals, but then you'll get 2 more the next week **from** those same 12 people you met with during the previous week. It's all about building up momentum.

Note: 12 appointments is the max that anyone AM should go on. If you try to schedule more than that, they end up running around too much and it reduces the quality they can bring to each appointment. If you have more than 12 appointments that can be set each week, it's time to consider hiring your second AM.

SALES TRAINING IS EVERYTHING
You must get **ongoing** sales training for your AM. I can't stress this enough. It doesn't matter how good he/she is. You can always get better at sales. Aren't you always trying to improve your marketing? Sales is no different. You should never just assume that your AM is great and, if the contract is to be gotten, they will get it. Not so.

> *"If you go out there and start making noise and making sales, people will find you. Sales cure all. You can talk about how great your business plan is and how well you are going to do. You can make up your own opinions, but you cannot make up your own facts. Sales cure all."*

> • *Daymond John, from Tim Ferriss's book "Tools of Titans"*

Imagine this scenario: You generate enough leads for your AM to schedule about 6 appointments per week. Your AM is converting about 1 in 6 to contracts, so you're getting about 1 contract per week, or 4 per month. You wish you had more money for marketing, but you don't. 6 appointments is the most you're able to schedule for the time being.

You add techniques like Advance Agreements, "Going for the No", and other elements that make up your Sales Process. You apply things you learned from the great sales books. These things add up, and instead of closing 1 in 6 customers, your AM starts bringing back 2 signed contracts for every 6 appointments.

What does that mean for you?

Well, it means you DOUBLED YOUR BUSINESS.

Notice that you didn't need to spend any additional money on marketing, analyze any additional leads, or go on any additional appointments. All you had to do was increase your **conversion rate**.

This is the kind of impact that sales training will have on your bottom line. It's the easiest money you can make. Learn to negotiate and everything in your business will get much better.

By this stage, you've overcome a major milestone. You've hired a great AM and they are ready to hit the ground running. But, your work has just begun. How you manage your AM has everything to do with the results you experience. This applies to the next 30 days, as well as the next 3 years. Develop your AM continually and you will reap rewards beyond your wildest dreams.

––––––

A Sales Coach I Recommend
Let me take this opportunity to introduce the very same sales coach that we hired for our own company, John Martinez.

There are a lot of sales coaches out there. Some are terrible. Some are fantastic. But, very few (if any) specialize in **real estate**. That's what attracted us to John.

John isn't just any sales coach. John is a sales coach *for* acquisition managers *for* real estate investing businesses. He understands the ins-and-outs of our businesses. He knows the struggles our AM's encounter, the objections they hear. He has specialized knowledge that you just won't get with a generic sales coach.

We hired John to come into our company for a handful of months, train our acquisition managers, and build out our Sales Process. The results were phenomenal. Our conversion rate on appointments doubled. Our sales reps were able to close deals without it feeling like they were pulling teeth. We began to focus much more on solving problems for our customers, versus just trying to talk them into signing contracts.

From a sales/customer experience perspective, everything feels much better since John came into our company.

To learn more about hiring John Martinez to train your AM, visit his website at:

http://midwestrev.com/

———

Chapter 5
NINJA SALES TRICKS TO GET MORE CONTRACTS

I mentioned that you need to start learning to sell right away. Whoever is meeting with sellers in your company must learn how to close!

Here are a few of the best sales tips that we use to get massive results. I'm only briefly describing them below. I encourage you to continue learning about these techniques beyond this book.

EXECUTING YOUR SALES PROCESS
When John Martinez, our sales coach, took a look at what we were doing, one of the first things he stressed is that we needed a "Sales Process". A Sales Process is simply a predetermined way of doing things that the sales rep follows each and every time. If they want to do something differently, they need to adjust it in the Sales Process and then it becomes part of the routine.

Let me give you an example of a Sales Process:

Step 1 - Build Rapport (Get seller to open up)
Step 2 - Diagnose (uncover emotion, their "why" behind wanting to sell)

Step 3 - Sell Benefit (make seller sell you on why they need you)

Step 4 - Set appointment with seller using Advance Agreements

Step 5 - Attend appointment with seller

Step 6 - Begin appointment with questions to uncover pain

Step 7 - Make Offer using Advance Agreements

Step 7 - Go for the No

Etc etc etc…

In a Sales Process, you never move on to the next step until the current step has been completed. If you can't build any rapport with a customer (i.e. get them to open up, start talking about themselves, something they're interested in, etc), then you don't move onto the Diagnosis phase. Jumping ahead in the sales process is a rookie move. It's really bad for sales.

Imagine trying that on a girl at the bar. She's standing at the bar, shoulders turned away from you. Her body language is telling you no. You try out some small talk and she straight up ignores you!

At that moment, would it make sense to blurt out "Hey, wanna go to my place?" Not unless you're an idiot, or really drunk. You're jumping ahead, and now you've really blown it with her and you're going home alone.

In sales, jumping ahead means going home alone, with no contracts. The relationships you have with the customer must follow the **natural process of healthy, human relationships**. The sales process is a sequential - you go from step 1, to 2, to 3, and so on. Just like you would in the dating world. This is because, at the deepest level, business and life are *one in the same*.

The above sales process is just an example. You need to get some sales training for you and your rep, decide what process you are going to follow, and then stick to it.

2 KEY BENEFITS OF HAVING A SALES PROCESS

There's two major benefits to having a Sales Process.

Benefit #1 - Accountability: Once you have a set process in place, you have something that you can hold your sales reps accountable to. As their manager, you need to listen to their calls and appointments and make sure they are following the process that you come up with.

Remember when I said not to jump ahead? The most common area that inexperienced reps do this is when it comes to making an offer. The sellers will also pressure them to jump to this step, because they want to know what you can pay.

If your AM gets on the first phone call with a customer and blurts out an offer of 50K during the first 5 minutes, the customer is probably going to hang up on them, unless they happen to want 50K for their property. And you know like I do that, in this business, what we can offer and what the seller wants is rarely in alignment.

That's why you have to follow a process that:

1) Brings their walls down
2) Allows them to trust you
3) Allows them to see the benefits you offer
4) Causes them to vocalize for themselves why they need your service and how it will relieve their pain, etc.

If you can accomplish this, price no longer becomes a barrier, because they see value in what you bring to the table **beyond** price. Critical stuff.

Benefit #2 - Consistency: Without a sales process, your rep will go on appointments and use different approaches every single time. Sometimes the AM will succeed, other times not. The problem is, you won't be able to pinpoint **where it went wrong** during the times when they fail.

Imagine if you sent out a direct mail campaign to 1,000 people, and on every single postcard you wrote a *different* message. 1,000 different people, 1,000 different messages. After the phone calls and leads came in, would you be able to analyze how that campaign did? Of course not. When the message is different every time, there's no way to know which ones worked, and which ones didn't. There's way too many variables at play.

This is essentially what will happen if you don't have a sales process, and if you don't regularly hold your AM accountable to *following* that process. You are giving your AM free roam to do as they please, both on the phone with sellers and at appointments. They will present a different version of your product/service every single time. There will be no constant variables that you can analyze.

Having a Sales Process fixes this because you can ask things like "so, at what point in the interaction did you lose the deal? When did the seller clam up and turn cold? At what stage in the process are you getting jammed up the most? Which part of the process makes you uncomfortable? Which questions are you having a hard time asking? What stage of the process seems to be destroying the rapport you've built with the customer" Then you can take a look at your Sales Process and identify steps that need to be added, removed, or tweaked.

You'll also uncover weaknesses in your AM. Many AM's are scared to complete certain parts of the Sales Process because they lack confidence or it feels unnatural to them. If you listen to recordings of their calls and appointments, you'll notice this. If you're a good manager, you'll ask them why it's happening and help them become more comfortable with doing it.

USING IPADS ON APPOINTMENTS

One thing we do, along with a lot of other investors, is use an iPad to give a presentation while on the appointment. I'll get to the main benefit of this in a minute, but here's some other reasons why your AM should use the iPad technique:

1) You can contain slides with market data that support the fact that it is a good time to sell.
2) You can play testimonial videos of previous satisfied customers
3) It gives the customer something to do (watch videos, etc) while you walk around doing your repair estimate
4) It gives off a professional vibe
5) It sets you apart from your competition
6) iPad's nowadays only cost around $300. If you get one extra deal it will pay for it many times over.
7) You can sync your iPad software with your database to instantly upload contracts, repair estimates, etc, to your primary database.

All of the above is great, but the best part about the iPad is that it can essentially contain, at a minimum, certain parts of your Sales Process. If one of your steps is "Uncovering Pain", you can have that as a slide that the seller sees. It's not going to kill the deal. In fact, it might actually show them that you care about more than just buying their house. It will also help beginner AM's stay on track (having a set of slides to go off of instead of winging it).

Build out the first version of your Sales Process. Don't over-think it. You'll be revising/updating it constantly anyways. Then, start to see how you can leverage technology to implement it and hold your AM accountable.

Just like you would test, track, and hold your marketing messages accountable to performance, you must do the same with your **established Sales Process.**

DIAGNOSE FIRST

When you go see a doctor, what happens? They ask a ton of questions and performs tests in order to collect information. Why? To make a diagnosis of the problem.

The role of an AM is the same. Step #1 is always diagnosis (After building rapport). Why did the customer call you? Why are they interested in selling? What benefit will selling the property bring to them? Why is that important to them? What emotion are they seeking to experience from getting that benefit? Why?

Can you see how asking these deeper questions gets to the real point of what's going on? This is how you effectively sell to someone. Selling is not about *you*. It's about *them*. You have to find out why it is important to them, and you can leverage that later when you start to talk about your product and its features. Notice I said "later", because you should never start blabbering about what you offer (especially not price) when you're still diagnosing the issue.

You will find, more often than you'd like, that there is not much to diagnose. The seller isn't really serious about selling, and they don't have a real problem they need to solve. That's when the next technique really comes in handy, because you can identify these people very early on and save valuable time and resources to apply elsewhere. That technique is called...

GOING FOR THE NO

Going for the No is a staple technique in the sales world, at least to those who know what they're doing. It's pretty counterintuitive and hard for new sales reps to adopt. Let me give you the brief summary here:

Going for the No simply means asking questions that easily allow your prospect to say "no". It gives them an easy out. I know you're already thinking that this sounds like a bad idea. Bear with me.

When you Go for the No, it doesn't mean that you are going to kill the deal. No means "not right now", it doesn't mean "never".

One of the secrets of Going for the No is that it more quickly gets you to a "yes". You need to weed through all of the people who aren't ready to sell right now. You can't afford to waste time finding out if someone is going to do business with you or not. In some scenarios, you can waste weeks, months, even YEARS finding out if a prospect is ever going to sell to you. Your time (or the AM's time) is way too precious. Going for the No means that you get *through* the no's faster, which means you get to the next *yes* that much faster, too.

Another big reason that Going for the No works is that it uses the "takeaway" principle. What you're essentially doing is "taking away" the thing that you had to offer the seller.

Psychologically, we don't like it when someone takes something away from us. Think of Shark Tank when one of the sharks makes an offer, then the entrepreneur kind of hesitates, and so the shark changes their mind and says "I'm out!".

The entrepreneurs are often devastated when this happens. When the offer was available, they were noncommittal and a bit indifferent to it. As soon as they were told they **can't** have the offer, they immediately changed their tone and desperately tried to win it back. This same thing happens in real estate. Your AM should never be afraid to take the offer "off the table", or to say the equivalent of "I'm out!".

Instead of trying to avoid "no's", the best sales reps make it a **goal** to get a certain number of "no's" everyday. This assures they are getting closer to a yes, while simultaneously weeding through the people who are not going to be a good fit to do business right now.

_____

GOING FOR THE NO QUESTIONS/STATEMENTS

Here's a few examples of "Going for the No":

"Hi Mike, I was just calling to let you know that I am going to close our file. You said you would get back to me. But, I haven't heard from you, so I'm assuming that we aren't a good fit?"

"So, it sounds like you have a nice property. You could have just listed it with a realtor. So why did you call me?"

"It doesn't seem like you are ready to commit to selling right now. I feel we might be wasting each others time here. Do you think that's fair to say?"

"I'm not going to be able to offer anywhere close to what you are asking. It doesn't seem like we should do business together, does it?"

"Why don't you just list your property with a realtor?"

_____

Using the above questions will be scary at first. You won't want to blow the deal. Many times, the above questions **will** result in the deal getting killed (not permanently, but for the time being). But here's the thing: that deal was going to get killed **anyways**, it's just that you were going to take 10 times longer to do it with your previous method. Use these questions and you'll see people's true colors much faster.

ADVANCE AGREEMENTS

Using Advance Agreements is a must. These are strategically placed questions that allow your AM to take and maintain control of the process the entire time.

Sandler training, a popular sales training program, calls Advance Agreements "Upfront Contracts".

When I was the AM for our company, one of my biggest frustrations was when a seller would stand me up. I'd do so much work running comps and preparing for our meeting, only to drive out there and meet no one.

Other times, they would show up. But, they were late, distracted, short, and/or uncooperative. All of which really messes up the effectiveness of a sales rep trying to do their job.

Another frustration I had was working with so many sellers who weren't ready to make a decision. Anyone who's ever been in sales understands this one. Most potential customers need to "think about it". That's the worst place to leave things in a salesperson/customer relationship. There's a very high chance you'll never see that person again.

Every time you end a phone call or an appointment, YOU must establish a very clear understanding of what will happen next.

It was only later that I learned that it was ME that was causing this confusion. I wasn't setting the expectation for them clearly enough, upfront. Advance Agreements is how your AM will do this.

Put another way: If you don't specifically tell your prospect that they **can't** do something, you don't have permission to get upset if they **do it**!

Advance Agreements help you maintain control of the process - even though it doesn't feel that way to the prospect because you get them to agree to it by using questions.

Here's some examples of Advance Agreement questions that need to become staples in the Sales Process of your AM. That means you hold them accountable to asking them. I think when you read them, this whole concept of the Advance Agreement will make a lot more sense.

———

Advance Agreement Examples Questions/Statements:
"When I come to your property, I'll need to run a repair estimate so I can give you the fairest offer possible. Once I do, I promise I won't leave the appointment without giving you an offer. Does that sound good to you?"

"I will make sure to let you know who we are, what we do, and provide you with all the information about our process. We can discuss these things for as long as it takes for you to feel comfortable. Does that sound fair to you?

"When I come to your property, I'll probably need about an hour to take a look at the place, run numbers, and discuss our options together. Does that work for you?"

"When I come out there, is there anything you'd like to discuss that we haven't yet covered on the phone?"

"I may need to ask you a few personal questions in order to get a better idea of what the best solution would be for your needs. Is that ok with you?"

"If I ask you a question that you aren't comfortable with, will you tell me that?"

"If I decide that I can buy your property, I will leave you with an exact offer, in contract form, before I go."

"If I agree to answer all of your questions, are you willing to do the same for me?"

"If you decide at any point that you don't want to work with me, or that you don't want to sell the house, will you tell me?"

"If I present you with a written offer during our appointment, will you be able to make a decision that day?

"Are you able to say yes to my offer if you like it?"

"Are you willing to give me a firm yes or no by the end of the day today?"

———

Notice how the above statements aren't how people "usually" talk. Instead, they take command and set clear expectations/next steps. People like this. They don't want to leave things unclear anymore than you do. Make sure you write your own Advance Agreement questions - or use the ones above - and put them in the appropriate places in your Sales Process.

MENTION PRICE = KILL THE DEAL

When you mention a number in this business, it changes everything.

Once you jump to price, it takes all the power away from you and puts it in your prospects hands. Your prospect no longer "needs you" because they believe that everything they need to make the decision is now in their hands (the contract, the price, the terms, etc). It's the shiny prize that you've been keeping close to your chest all along. Once you hand it over, the ball is no longer in your court.

Also, prospects aren't as cooperative once they "know your number" because they now have the ability to shop your proposal to the highest bidder.

Therefore, the MOST IMPORTANT Advance Agreement happens right before you give your offer. You must get your customer to agree that he will give you a firm yes or no, within an agreed-upon time frame.

Here's an example of how that might go down:

AM: "Now Mr. Seller, I'm about to make you an offer in writing. Let me ask you this question. Have I been cooperative and upfront with you throughout this process?

Mr. Seller: "Yes"

AM: When I give you this offer, are you willing to do the same for me?

Mr. Seller: "Yes"

AM: Ok. What is a fair time frame for you to review this offer and give me a firm yes or no?

Mr. Seller: "By tomorrow"

AM: "That sounds good. What time tomorrow?"

Mr. Seller: "Noon"

AM: "Ok, so do we have an agreement that you will call me before noon tomorrow and give me a firm yes or no?"

Mr. Seller: "Yes"

AM: "Great. Here's the offer…"

Notice how taking about 1 minute to frame the offer differently and position yourself makes all the difference. Compare this with what most AM's do. They hand the customer an offer and cower in a corner for 2 weeks hoping that today will be the day the customer finally calls them back.

I hope you can now see that the sales process, and its contents, are everything.

Chapter 6
GETTING YOUR AM MORE LEADS TO WORK

Do you need more for your AM to do? Are you worried that you'll hire this person and you won't have any leads for them to work?

This is a common concern for investors who haven't hired an AM yet. I totally understand it. Here's some tips to make sure they have a full plate.

WORK YOUR DATABASE LEADS

When I say "database", I'm referring to the leads you already have in-house, those that you personally generated through direct mail, internet, referral, etc. Those are usually the best leads and should be treated like gold. Have your AM follow up with all your database leads at least once per month. Over time, as you get a lot of leads in your database, you'll need to bucket off a portion of only the hottest leads for the AM to work.

We use a "Property Score" system to rate the quality of leads as they come in, based upon price, motivation, location, condition, etc. Our AM only works the leads with a high property score.

BUILD YOUR REFERRAL NETWORK

I think this is a marketing responsibility upfront but once it's built, you can hand it off to the AM. What you want to do is build a list of all of the types of people shown below. Always be building that list. Once you have it, you need to communicate with them regularly. A short email every Tuesday morning saying "Got anything? I have cash and am ready to buy" will suffice. You can send the same email out to everyone all at once, BCC style so they don't see each other's email addresses. It's free to do and your AM will stay top-of-mind with other people in the industry who have eyes on available deals.

Here's the types of people to put on your email list:

1) Wholesalers
2) Property Managers
3) Attorneys
4) Investors
6) Title Companies
7) Realtors

I actually recommend building your referral list one "type" at a time. For example, choose only property managers and try to get every property manager in your city on your list. You need to pick up the phone and call them initially. Then once that's complete, move onto wholesalers, etc...

MAKE LOTS OF OFFERS!

Initially, this is also Marketing Manager responsibility. That may be you, or you may have hired someone to do this. Either way, someone needs to set up systems that mine the following databases for properties that are for sale:

1) FSBO
2) MLS
3) Craigslist
4) Zillow
5) Auction

Mine these websites for the types of deals that fit your criteria. I doubt you're going to be making offers on $800,000 brand new houses. Put the ones you DO want on a spreadsheet and get them to your AM so that they can work them like any other lead - making phone calls, setting and attending appointments, and making offers.

Yes, the properties found on these channels are going to be "colder", meaning less likely to sell at a discount. Many other investors are looking at the deals out there on these public channels. Most of them are also writing them off as bad deals.

I can say from personal experience that when I list my own properties for sale, I don't always get a lot of offers. Even in a hot market. Anytime I get any offer, it gets my attention. Don't be the guy who assumes "he'll never take my offer". Submit it and see what happens. At the very least, you'll be noticed. Plus, since we have email these days, you don't have to actually mail anything or spend money to make an offer. It's free!

If you're thinking of sending people contracts, I recommend sending a Letter of Intent (LOI) instead. LOI's are not formal, legal contracts, they're just a professional expression of your intent to make an offer, assuming the repair inspection checks out. People take these a lot more seriously than just an email or a comment made over the phone. Use LOI's because you really need to see the property and run a repair estimate before you can make a real offer. The LOI gives them a ballpark offer and shows that you are truly interested.

MAKE SELLER FINANCING OFFERS

If one of your goals is to acquire rental properties, you need to train your AM to make seller financing (or owner financing) offers. This is where you structure the offer with terms, and the seller becomes the lender on the deal. It prevents you from having to go to a bank to get a loan on a house. I know guys who have 100+ properties that they got solely from seller financing deals. They never once had to go to a bank, and often times, they didn't have to come out of pocket very much either. Add this one tool to your toolbelt and you'll explode your portfolio. My friend Matt Theriault is really well-versed in this space and I'd wholeheartedly recommend his training to learn how to do this.

Chapter 7

USING YOUR AM AS THE TRANSACTION COORDINATOR

What is a transaction coordinator you say? This is the person that coordinates the transaction *post-contract*. So from the moment the contract is signed, they work with the title company to see it through to closing.

LIST OF DUTIES FOR THE TC

Transaction Coordinator duties include:

1) Sending the contract to the title company and requesting to start the title search
2) Following up w/ title company to check on status of title search
3) Calling seller to keep them updated on the status of the closing
4) Calling seller to get documents like insurance releases, death certificates, etc.
5) Scheduling inspections/contractors with seller and other parties
6) Scheduling actual closing w/ the seller and title company

7) Clouding titles when necessary (recording the contract) with the county, to prevent a seller from selling the property to someone else behind your back once they've already signed a contract with you, when you've spent money and resources seeing that deal through to closing.
8) Reviewing closing documents
9) Signing for you (you can use a one-time resolution/POA for each property and avoid having to go to title company)
10) Giving sellers a ride to the title company
11) Picking up keys from title company once sale is completed
12) Following up with title company to make sure wire/checks are received after closing is completed

In the event that you can't be there, I'd recommend using your AM to also actually *attend* inspections/contractor visits at properties you have under contract. It's good for someone to meet any type of vendor at the property and you as the owner may not have time to be at all of these appointments.

Chapter 8
USING YOUR AM AS THE INSPECTOR

I made this a separate chapter because I'm hoping to help you avoid some major "repair estimate" mistakes that I've made in my career.

HOW TO AVOID MY BIGGEST MISTAKE
When we first got started, we knew nothing about houses. We would walk through a property, glance around, and if there wasn't a hole in the kitchen floor, we thought it was a nice house. We never sought out any proper training on how to inspect a property, identify repairs needed, and properly estimate the costs of those repairs.

It felt like there was so much to learn that we just kind of ignored it. It wasn't until we actually BOUGHT the house that we started to learn all of the dirty details. At that point we had a contractor going through it and giving us bids. One time we discovered foundation issues in 3 of our rehab projects **all within the same week!** It was a big mess.

Even in the event that we DID get a contractor estimate and inspection before we bought the house, there was still a big problem. We'd offer Mr. Seller $80,000 for the house, and then the contractor bid would come in with $15,000 in additional repairs that we hadn't seen. We would either have to go back to Mr. Seller and tell him that we now could only pay $65,000 for his house, or just cancel the deal all together. That route just resulted a big waste of Mr. Seller's time and energy, and he was understandably not very happy about it.

So, in an attempt to solve that issue, we started to have our AM's run repair estimates **during** the appointment. We'd say to them "OK, we can pay up to 70K for that house, **minus repairs**". Then if the AM found 10K in repairs, he knew that the most he could offer Mr. Seller was 60K. That dialed in our offers a lot more and prevented us from misleading the customer. But, there was still a big problem.

Neither we nor our AM really knew how to properly identify repairs needed. I mean, there's a lot going on in a house. There's multiple systems that need to be examined. Even certified home inspectors miss things all the time, and they admit that. So you're never going to be perfect. You're always going to miss things. But, because it's such a daunting task, you've got to sharpen your skills. You have to get as good as you can possibly be at this part of the business.

WHY YOU SHOULD GET YOUR AM CERTIFIED AS A HOME INSPECTOR

I recommend you go ahead and get your AM certified as a home inspector. It only takes a couple weeks at most and doesn't cost a ton. Check out Nachi.org to see what the certification requirements are for home inspectors in your state. Home inspection courses will make your AM ten times more qualified to inspect properties than he/she was before getting certified. Imagine the cost/reward on that kind of investment. You might even consider getting the certification yourself.

But wait, there's more! Not only will they be much more likely to spot defects in the properties they visit, but you can also use their qualification as an inspector to get them in the door with customers. Offering a discounted or completely free home inspection is a great way to get in the door with a potential customer. Once your AM reveals all the problems with the property and provides that customer with the inspection report, the customer is more likely to want to just get rid of it. Plus, they got something of value from you for free, so they feel a bit indebted to you. That's when your AM can come in and offer to purchase. This is more of a marketing strategy blended with sales, but it can work wonders for your company.

Chapter 9
CLOSING THOUGHTS

ALWAYS BE HIRING

This book has instructed you on how to hire, train, and leverage an AM for maximum results. In closing, I want to mention this: you should **always** be hiring. OK, so not actually hiring, but staying prepared to hire. What does this mean? Run your job posting at least once per month. Collect applications. You can create a generic reply that tells them the position has been filled but you've kept their names in case something opens up.

What does this do? In essence it creates a "bench" (like the bench on a sports team) of hungry, qualified AM's, in the event that your AM quits or does not perform up to your standards. It takes 30-90 days to hire an AM, and if you lose yours, you definitely don't want to go that long without someone meeting with sellers and making offers. It could have a huge negative impact on your business. Having a list of pre-qualified candidates to call right away dramatically shortens the hiring timeline.

Most sales managers hang onto their marginal performers longer than they should. They justify this by saying things like "Oh he'll come around" or "Well I need someone to do the job". Don't be this guy! You have to be tough. Firing people is the least comfortable part of being a business owner. But I've got news for you. It's part of the job. If you have a 100% retention rate at your company, you're being too soft. Not everyone you hire is going to be a perfect fit. Recognize this and take action as soon as possible. If you've set clear goals upfront and they aren't meeting those goals, getting fired should come as no surprise to them.

You could even go as far as lining up a "backup AM" in the event that your AM goes on vacation, gets sick, or gets too bogged down with appointments occasionally. Someone to "pick up the slack". This is because your ultimate goal should be...

HIRING ADDITIONAL AM'S

Once your AM is going on 10-12 appointments regularly each week, and you feel like you could book another 6-10 because of all the leads you've got, it's time to hire your second AM. This is an awesome milestone in your business because you have two full-time people out in the field getting contracts signed.

Plus, it generates competition between the two AM's. Each week, it's like a contest to see who can get the most contracts signed. Getting to the stage where you can justify having two AM's will be huge for your business. Remember that this comes from marketing. The more leads you generate, the more reps you'll need.

You now have everything you need to make this life-changing shift in your business. If you're still resisting the idea of hiring someone, go back and answer the "resistance questions" in Chapter 1. What's the worst that could happen? What's the best that could happen? Does the risk/reward ratio make sense?

I want to thank each and every one of you who took the time to read this book. This information is something I've wanted to share for a while, because I feel that it's one of the biggest secrets to having a successful real estate investing business.

If you're interested in working with me further in a one-on-one or group coaching setting, visit my website for more information at:

http://www.brianellwood.net/get-coaching/

Thanks again. I hope we cross paths in the future. Till then!

Brian Ellwood

RESOURCES

Here's all the resources I mentioned throughout the book.

Never Split the Difference - Fantastic Sales Book

https://www.tonyrobbins.com/disc/ - Free DISC Test

Nachi.org - Home Inspection Certification in Your State

John Martinez - Amazing sales coach

Podio - Recommended CRM

Slack - Recommended communication channel for all internal team members

Voxer - Walkie Talkie app for communicating with AM and rest of team

AUTHOR BIOGRAPHY

Brian Ellwood spent most of his childhood growing up near Nashville, Tennessee. After graduating from the University of Tennessee and spending a total of 15 years in dead end jobs, Brian turned to real estate. He started his first real estate investing business in 2011. Brian's company now does over 70 fix n' flips per year in Middle Tennessee and owns a portfolio of rental properties. Brian lives in Denver and manages his team and his projects virtually. Brian is also a real estate investing coach, teaching others how to build virtual real estate businesses in any market and create a portfolio of low-risk rental properties that generate passive income.

Made in the USA
Monee, IL
15 May 2021

68743104R00049